"*Let us be silent, that we may hear the whispers of the gods.*"

— *Ralph Waldo Emerson*

Let Time Stand Still

On your most stressful days, unwind with a bath before bed. Prepare your bedroom before you get in the tub; pull down the covers, lower the lights, take care of last minute household duties. Use your favorite bath ingredients and soak for at least 15 minutes. Breathe in relaxation and let your mind lose the visual stresses of the past day. Towel off and use a body lotion. Climb into bed for a restful night's sleep.

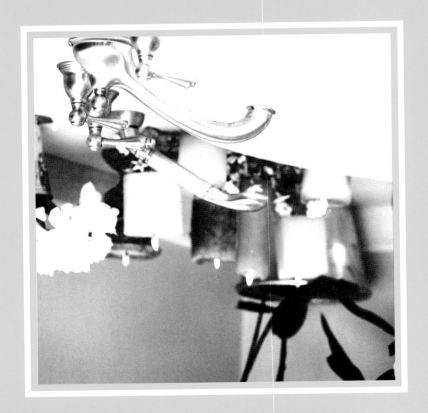

Luxury can be as simple as lighting a scented candle, drawing a bath, and locking the door.

The lush beauty of nature restores our sense of calm. Bring nature within your reach.

Your inner balance is restored through friends, family, and attachments to life building relationships.

Unwind with an Out-of-Body Experience.

Share your life lessons with a friend.

To pamper yourself in the shower, switch the showerhead to one that imitates a natural rain shower. These are wider heads that simulate showering in the outdoors. The water droplets gently pour over your body and naturally stimulate your skin. A fine suggestion for those of us who don't have the option to bathe out of doors.

Set the mood for your bath by dimming the lights, choosing tranquil music, and turning off the phone. Run the bath water to be a bit warmer than body temperature.

Natural mineral salts are derived from ancient seabeds. These offer a concentration of minerals that, combined with natural oils, can be very therapeutic.

Soaking in a warm tub allows your skin to absorb moisturizing ingredients and essential oils that may also invigorate and refresh you.

Try bathing with your sweetheart to unwind after a long day. Unplug your clock, your phone, and any other connections to the outside world that may interrupt you. Light a candle, add your favorite bath bubbles, and enjoy time away from this chaotic world.

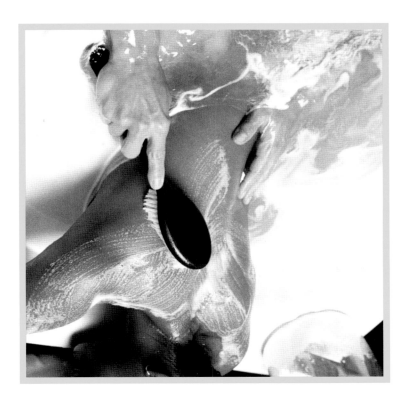

The scents of aromatherapy harmonize your body. Try lavender to promote a relaxing night's sleep or rosemary to increase circulation.

A tub full of bubbles is a luxury everyone can afford. Select bubbles that are made with natural products. The bubbles will be smaller but your skin will be moisturized instead of dried out.

Getaway? Put a cucumber on your eyes, breathe deeply, and put your feet up in the middle of the day.

Ease into
Tranquility

*B*lur the boundaries between fantasy and reality with the scent and power of ancient spa treatments.

*R*adiant beauty rises from the undiscovered places within you.

Using essential aromatherapy oils in your bath water gives you several benefits. The oils emit fragrance. When you inhale the fragrance it is believed the oils may change your state of mind in a positive way. While still in the tub, massage the oil into your skin. The oil will subtly absorb and promote lustrous skin.

Listen carefully and you will begin to hear that still, small voice within that is you.

A Japanese custom before bathing is to shower before you take a bath. This ensures a more hygienic soak and also heightens the relaxation factor.

Self-healing begins with the balance between your diet and your emotions.

Linger in your bath until your mood lightens and you feel your inner balance restored. Meditate on bliss. What does it mean to you? Where have you found it? How did you feel? Make this moment a turning point for you.

After working in the garden steep your hands in a bath of lavender oil to invigorate tired, aching muscles.

Our body resonates when cared for with love, patience, and thoughtful devotion. Take a few moments to soak your feet in a tub of sea salts, then gently scrub off dead skin. Finish with a body lotion. You'll be amazed at how many times during the day your feet will thank you.

Sensual pleasures are a key to de-stressing your body. Unwind with the scent of sandalwood, taste the pure fruit goodness of a tangerine, touch the pure oil of peppermint, close your eyes, listen to the sound of the waves crashing onto a beach.

Ayurveda is an ancient Indian holistic technique. Ayurveda specialists suggest using oil on your body before you bathe to allow the oil to fully saturate your skin. Once a week, massage oil into your skin 3-4 hours before you bathe. Choose from olive, coconut, sesame or almond oil.

What is the jewel in your crown? Your body jewel? Take care of it. For an inexpensive bath treatment, try using milk in your bath. Ayurveda technique suggests using milk in the bath to soften the skin. Pour 1 cup of milk in a separate bowl and rub it over your wet body. Rinse in the tub. Feel the silky difference.

A loofah sponge is a plant that grows in tropical climates. Try the loofah in place of a cloth to delicately cleanse your skin. Rejuvenate!

Do you love the scent of roses? Sprinkle rose petals into your bath water. The natural scent soothes the senses into a blur of quiet repose.

Bath salts draw toxins from the surface of the skin and soften the bath water. Ease yourself into your bath. Enjoy the gentle exfoliation and the calm, relaxing mood that overtakes your body.

Renew your inner balance

Unravel your daily stress with silence and meditation.

Taking care of yourself is time well spent. Even if your life is harried and confusing, you need to take a few minutes out of each day to relax and focus on yourself. Find out what exhilaration you keep with you from your time in the bath. What anchors you and keeps you centered even in the eye of the storm?

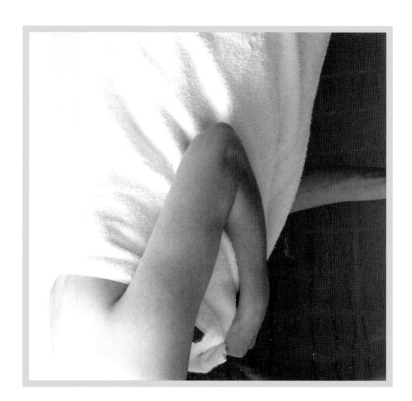

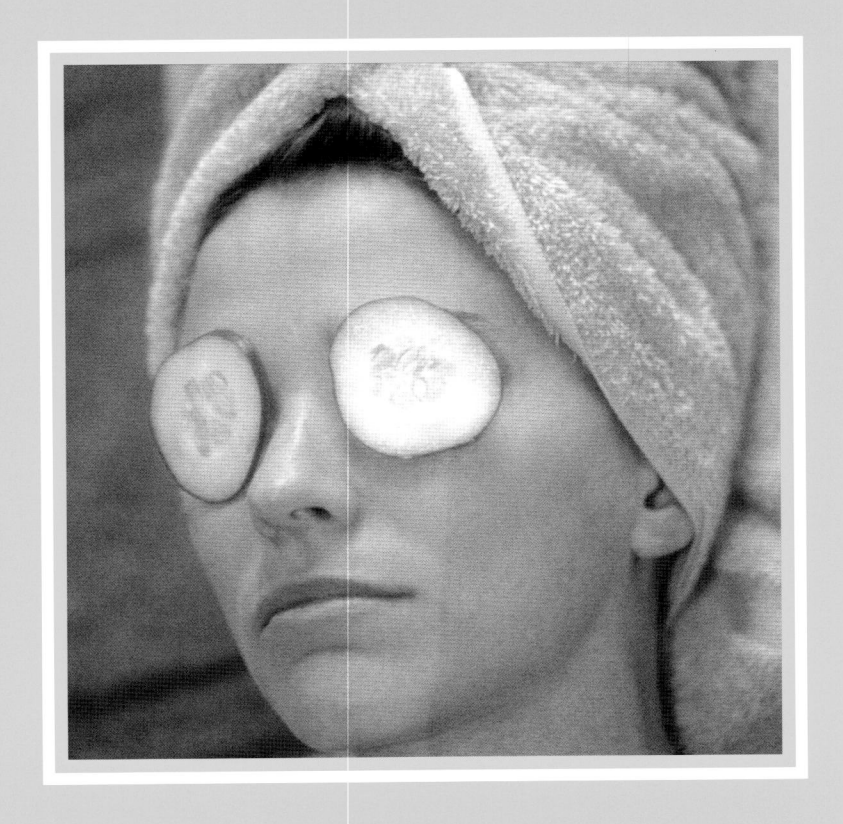

We always have the choice to connect to something deeper within ourselves. Mud baths were originally used in ancient times for purifying and detoxifying the body. At home, you can use a mud treatment on your face to relax those tiny muscles. It will also soften your skin, a beneficial effect to spreading the mud mask on your face.

We always have the choice to connect to something deeper within ourselves.

A transcending moment becomes that in which you define your life. You begin to reach for it every day.

© 2004 Havoc Publishing
San Diego, California
U.S.A.

Text by Maureen Webster

ISBN 0-7416-4114-3

www.havocpub.com

Made in China